Praise for *Visit the Sick*

What do pastors do when they visit the sick? Brian Croft has written a marvelous piece to assist us. His work is theologically grounded, gospel centered, and full of practical wisdom. I recommend it enthusiastically.

Thomas R. Schreiner, James Buchanan Harrison professor of New Testament interpretation at The Southern Baptist Theological Seminary and teaching pastor at Clifton Baptist Church

Visitation is a timely topic for pastors and Christians today. And Brian Croft hits the mark. He provides sensitive, God-honoring, and gospel-driven counsel to pastors and Christians. If you're like me — someone who feels ill-equipped to say the right words or do the right things at someone's sickbed — you'll delight in this book.

Thabiti Anyabwile, senior pastor of First Baptist Church, Grand Cayman, and author of The Faithful Preacher

"What should I say? How long should I stay? Why should I go? What should I pray? What if the person is dying? What if they're not a Christian?" These are just a few of the many apprehensions people have about visiting the sick. Brian Croft gives practical assistance that should eliminate feelings of inadequacy and motivate us to fulfill Christ's commission, "I was sick and you visited me." A biblically based, highly practical manual for Christian caregivers, this insightful book can be read in just a few minutes, but its down-to-earth counsel will equip you to confidently visit the sick for years to come.

Bob Russell, former senior pastor of Southeast Christian Church, Louisville, Kentucky

Seldom does one encounter pastoral resources of a practical nature that are richly biblical and theologically grounded. Brian Croft's excellent book provides more than a mere "how-to" guide for pastoral visitation. He offers the gospel of grace and power needed for the kind of practical help that brings honor to God and leads people to Christ. Filled with wisdom and rooted in theology, this resource offers the blend that is so needed in the church today.

Bruce A. Ware, professor of Christian theology at The Southern Baptist Theological Seminary and author of God's Lesser Glory

Many pastors and church leaders spend time visiting the sick. Some feel that their visits are fruitful times of ministry; others feel very awkward. Very few people, however, have the intuitive people skills and the pastoral expertise to do this successfully without some training. Read *Visit the Sick* for yourself, study it as a staff, or use it as a training resource for all those in your church who regularly visit the sick. It can help turn a routine responsibility into a time of effective ministry.

> *Donald Whitney, associate professor of biblical spirituality*
> *at The Southern Baptist Theological Seminary and author*
> *of* Spiritual Disciplines of the Christian Life

Many younger pastors (and not so young ones as well) have never received the sort of practical guidance that Brian Croft gives in *Visit the Sick*. It will now be a recommended text in my pastoral ministries class, and I heartily commend it to others.

> *Ray Van Neste, PhD, associate professor*
> *of Christian studies and director of the R. C. Ryan Center*
> *for Biblical Studies, Union University*

Times of suffering from sickness have the power to prepare the heart for the seed of the word as few other things can. Brian Croft has done an excellent job of showing how the pastor can make the word of God central in his ministry to the sick and dying.

> *Dr. Andrew Davis, senior pastor of First Baptist Church in*
> *Durham, North Carolina, and author of*
> An Approach to Extended Memorization of Scripture

Brian Croft has given us a practical and theological guide to caring for our congregations. It is a must-read for those interested in a theology for visiting the sick.

> *Dr. George D. Barnett, ministry resource consultant*
> *for the Georgia Baptist Convention*

VISIT THE SICK

REVISED AND UPDATED

**Ministering God's Grace
in Times of Illness**

BRIAN CROFT

ZONDERVAN

ZONDERVAN

Visit the Sick
Copyright © 2014 by Brian Croft

Previously published in 2008 by Day One Publications under the same title.

This title is also available as a Zondervan ebook.
Visit www.zondervan.com/ebooks.

Requests for information should be addressed to:

Zondervan, 3900 *Sparks Dr. SE, Grand Rapids, Michigan* 49546

Library of Congress Cataloging-in-Publication Data

Croft, Brian.
    Visit the sick : ministering God's grace in times of illness / Brian
Croft.
        p. cm. — (Practical shepherding series)
    ISBN 978-0-310-51714-6
    1. Church work with the sick. I. Title.
BV4335.C76 2014
259'.4—dc23   2013042722

Cover design and illustrations: Jay Smith-Juicebox Designs
Interior design: Matthew Van Zomeren

Printed in the United States of America

HB 05.02.2019

To my father,
who taught me the value of this work
through many visits and house calls with his patients —
thank you for graciously allowing me to accompany you —

&

In loving memory of Ferrill Gardner,
known by those who knew him best as
"the master of the hospital room".

CONTENTS

Foreword by Mark Dever. 9

INTRODUCTION 11

Chapter 1
GOD'S CARE FOR THE SICK:
BIBLICAL THEOLOGY. 15

Chapter 2
SPIRITUAL CARE FOR THE SICK:
THEOLOGICAL PRECISION 29

Chapter 3
WISE CARE FOR THE SICK:
PASTORAL IMPLICATIONS 39

Chapter 4
SKILLED CARE FOR THE SICK:
PRACTICAL NECESSITIES 48

Chapter 5
COMMUNITY CARE FOR THE SICK:
EQUIPPING THE SAINTS 55

CONCLUSION 60

Afterword by William V. Croft, MD 63

Acknowledgments 65

Appendix 1: CHECKLIST Visit the Sick: Theological,
  Pastoral, and Practical Categories. 67

Appendix 2: Spiritual Conversations 68

Appendix 3: FAQ 73

Appendix 4: "Sickness" by J. C. Ryle (Abridged Version) 80

Bibliography 92

Notes 93

FOREWORD

I REMEMBER THE FIRST TIME I did hospital visitation. I was twenty-one or twenty-two. I had just begun to work in a church, and the senior pastor asked me to visit some older members in the hospital. And let me make it clear. These were older members. I mean, as in "born in the previous century" older! I didn't know any of them. They certainly wouldn't know me. What would I have to give them? What could I contribute to them? The deep and self-conscious awkwardness of feeling useless came over me.

God was very kind to me in that first day of visitation. And over the weeks and months to come, I made many more visits to that hospital and others on the north shore of Boston. Oh, how I wish then that this little book had existed! What frustration it might have saved me! What embarrassment it might have saved me! How it would have served those I was trying to encourage.

Brian Croft is well qualified to help the pastor in this way. He is a faithful pastor, himself accustomed to visiting the sick in the hospital. I've known Brian for a number of years now. His father, Bill Croft, is a physician and a wonderful Christian man. So Brian has grown up around those who show concern for the sick. His brother, Scott Croft, has served on staff with me at the Capitol Hill Baptist Church in Washington, DC, and for years served as the chairman of our elders. Scott has been an encouragement to, instructor to, and student of Brian. Brian's sister, Beth Spraul, is a member of our congregation and has served in hospital chaplaincies. So, from many angles, Brian is a man well suited to advise us in these matters.

In this little volume, Brian helps us to think straightforwardly and faithfully about God's truth and God's people. His advice is as sound as it is simple. Some parts of this may be about matters you've already figured out. But isn't it better to be told something twice than not at all? Let Brian's be that reinforcing voice. And don't be surprised if you read some things that you hadn't thought of before. Read this book, and let Brian help you in helping others.

Mark Dever, senior pastor of Capitol Hill
Baptist Church, Washington, DC

INTRODUCTION

WE ARE VICTIMS OF OUR OWN CULTURE. The twenty-first century has brought with it demands, pressures, and deadlines that have left us feeling as if our lives are often spinning out of control. We have all felt the tension of time with God, work, family, church, school, social occasions, house repairs, personal errands, and sleep, all of which need our daily attention. Unfortunately, we often come to the end of the day—and we're exhausted, and we wonder where the time went. Our day becomes reminiscent of the hamster running in his wheel—busy, but going nowhere. It is this tension that leads to the neglect of certain essential responsibilities in the life of a Christian. One of those essential tasks is the visiting and care of the sick within our own churches.

My goal for this book is to instruct and motivate us to recapture this God-honoring practice, and to do so by reaching for a standard that, frankly, is foreign to us today. This means we must be taught by those who lived at a different time within a different culture. We must learn from those who modeled an astounding dedication to this call. We must learn from their accounts and convictions. We must be instructed by our heroes from church history.

Maybe the greatest historical example of visiting the afflicted was the seventeenth-century Puritan pastor Richard Baxter. Baxter had an amazing strategy to visit not just the sick but everyone in his congregation throughout the English town of Kidderminster regularly and faithfully. In the midst of his highly disciplined routine, Baxter developed a certain sensitivity to those in his congregation who were sick and homebound. He writes in *The Reformed Pastor*, "We must be diligent in visiting the sick, and helping them to prepare either for a fruitful life, or a happy death."[1]

Many others in Baxter's time and beyond were found to be diligent in this task; yet as America made its turn into the twentieth century, the local church and its priorities began to change. As the United States grew into an industrialized nation, this led to changes in the church, and sadly, pastoral care for the sick became more of an afterthought in many churches. Healthy models of pastors who are known for their care for the sick are few and far between today. To aid us in recapturing this lost and forgotten practice, we will look beyond the twentieth century at historical models that will help us to care for the sick in a way that glorifies God in our day.

There are, of course, several challenges in taking this approach. Our culture has changed, and our lives today are quite different from the lives of the Puritans whom Baxter pastored. Instead of simply copying his model, we will look at some of the key principles underlying his practice and try to paint a picture of what these principles look like when applied today. Pastors like Baxter and Spurgeon would have had no categories to relate to the hypersensitive, self-consumed privacy mind-set we find rampant in our twenty-first-century culture. So some adjustments need to be made with regard to the practicality of visiting hospitals, nursing homes, rehabilitation centers, and homes.

Before considering the practical details of visiting the sick, you may need to be convinced that this task is important for pastors, as well as for the members of a local church. We will begin by taking a moment to consider why care for the sick should be a priority in our lives.

First of all, it is biblical. James exhorts those who are sick to call for the elders of the church to pray over them (James 5:14). Even non-elders were encouraged to pray in a similar manner (James 5:16). And it was Jesus who taught and modeled this practice of caring for the sick. He indicated that it was a primary way to show love to him and our brother (Matthew 25:36, 40). Jesus led by example (Mark 1:31). The apostles also followed this pattern of caring for the sick (Acts 3:7; 28:8). Widows, especially, were to be cared for (1 Timothy 5:3 – 10). Caring for the sick was one aspect of caring for souls, something for which leaders will give an account (Hebrews 13:17). Though this is a quick listing of some passages, it is clear that Jesus and the apostles cared about the sick and afflicted, and they exhorted others to do so as well.

Visiting the sick is also a tremendous opportunity to minister to and to love our fellow Christians. Charles Spurgeon wisely states, "I venture to say that the greatest earthly blessing that God can give to any of us is health, with the exception of sickness. Sickness has frequently been of more use to the saints of God than health has."[2] A spiritual attentiveness that accompanies sickness often fizzles when we are in good health. As we care for one other, we must learn to seize the moments that God in his kindness provides for our spiritual growth and nurture — even moments of suffering in the midst of sickness.

We must also recognize that the ministry of the care and visitation of the sick is not limited to pastors and leaders in the church, but is the calling of all — singles and married, men and women. Even families can practice this ministry together. Similar to the early church's dedication to provide for the needs of the church (Acts 2; 4), we must see this as the calling and responsibility of all members of a local church to one another. Visiting those who are sick and afflicted can have a powerful impact on the lives of those who practice this ministry. The nineteenth-century Scottish pastor David Dickson writes, "On the bed of sickness the Lord ripens his people for glory, and to the elder himself it is often a scene of instruction and revival."[3] God will not only sanctify the sick through sickness but also teach and encourage the healthy who offer care, prayer, and encouragement. My hope and prayer for you is that you will mature in your love for God and for others in the body of Christ as you answer God's call to care for the sick.

CHAPTER 1

GOD'S CARE FOR THE SICK

Biblical Theology

"I was sick and you looked after me."
Matthew 25:36

AS CHRISTIANS, WE VIEW OUR LIVES through the lens of the Bible because it is the foundation of who we are and all that we know about God. Misunderstandings about God and his purposes can be directly linked to a failure to know the full story line of the Bible. If we wish to correctly interpret the Bible for our individual lives, we must learn to read and understand the Bible in its full context of redemptive history.

The aim of this chapter is to help you understand God's purposes as they unfold in the story line of the Bible, particularly in relation to sickness, disease, and suffering. The reality that we live in a world marred by sickness and disease is evident throughout Scripture. Yet we need to know more than just a collection of verses in the Bible on this subject. We need to grasp how God is working out his purposes through sickness, disease, and suffering, all for the good of his people and his own glory. The progression of Scripture from Genesis to Revelation contains an unfolding story line that reveals two key themes: God is sovereign over sickness and healing, and God calls his people to care for the needy and afflicted.

Creation

The Bible begins its historical narrative with a world that is foreign to us today. We read that God created the heavens, the earth, and all the living creatures (Genesis 1–2). He also created man and woman in his image (Genesis 1:27) and "saw all that he had made, and it was very good" (Genesis 1:31). God placed the man and woman in the Garden of Eden, where they were given the task of ruling over his creation and told to be fruitful and increase in number. The garden was beautiful, and in it there flowed a river to water the garden and a tree of life that was good for food (Genesis 2:9–10). This was a world that was perfectly made—man was created in the image of God, man enjoyed unhindered fellowship with God, and man ruled over the creation while fully submitting to God's rule over them.

In this world there was an absence of sickness, pain, disease, suffering, and affliction. No cancer preyed on these first human bodies. No aches and pains plagued them. There were no diseases to be healed, nor any sickness that needed to be cured. Most significantly, there was no death. All was good, perfect, and right, as God intended for his creation.

Fall

This world, the world of Genesis 1–2, is not the same world we live in today. There is one significant difference. Today we experience sickness, disease, and death. There is clearly something really wrong with the world we live in and with those who were made in God's image. The changes we find in our world today can be traced back to Genesis 3, where we see that Adam and Eve sinned by disobeying God's word in eating of the tree of the knowledge of good and evil and suffered the consequences (Genesis 3:6). God had told Adam and Eve not to eat from this tree or they would die (Genesis 2:17). Satan tempted Eve, and she ate from the tree and gave some of its fruit to her husband (Genesis 3:6). Instead of obeying God's command, they rebelled against him. They wanted to rule rather than be ruled by God's commands and boundaries.

As a result of man's sin and rebellion, the curse of death that God warned of came on them and all of his creation. On that day, sin and its consequences entered the world. Adam and Eve were removed from the garden and barred from access to the tree of life, whose fruit would grant them eternal life (Genesis 3:22). Now there would be pain in childbirth (Genesis 3:16). Man's task to work and rule over the creation became hard and painful. There now existed a great separation from their once-unhindered fellowship with God. Most significantly, death entered the world with their sin, and as a result, man would suffer not just physical death but also the effects of death—old age, pain, and suffering.

Here we learn that sickness and disease are part of the curse, the result of human disobedience and sin. Today you can find many scientific explanations for what sickness is and why it exists in our world. But the Bible offers a simple and straightforward answer. Sickness, disease, pain, suffering, affliction, and death are all undeniable evidences that we have rebelled against God and fallen from our original calling. They reveal our desperate need for redemption. We quickly learn from the narrative that only a sovereign, eternal God can intervene to save the creation from this curse. The hope of the gospel, which includes the promise of physical resurrection, begins to unfold in a glorious work of redemption, one that will culminate in the death and resurrection of God's own Son, Jesus Christ.

The Life of Israel

Thankfully, the story is far from over at this point. God plans to redeem mankind through a chosen nation that will be his people among all the other nations of the earth. This nation was promised to Abraham (Genesis 12) through a child, Isaac, who would be born in Abraham's old age (Genesis 21). From this child, the nation of Israel (Jacob, Isaac's child) would begin. With Isaac's grandson, Joseph, the nation of Israel relocated to Egypt, where they multiplied greatly (Exodus 1:7), eventually becoming enslaved to the Egyptians. Again, we see God's sovereign purpose at work. Hundreds of years before their enslavement, God promised (Genesis 15:13–14) that he would deliver his people from their oppression and judge the nation holding them captive. Through the events of this deliverance, God uses sickness and disease to save his people and reveal his glory.

Moses goes to Pharaoh and demands that he free God's people from their enslavement. Pharaoh refuses, which leads to a series of judgments on the Egyptians. Several of these judgments involve diseases that fall on the livestock and painful sores on the people (Exodus 9). The ultimate judgment that falls on Pharaoh is the death of all firstborn children (Exodus 12). God inflicts disease as judgment on the Egyptians and uses it to protect his people, Israel. This use of disease as *judgment on sin* helps us understand why God later says to his people, "If you listen carefully to the LORD your God and do what is right in his eyes, if you pay attention to his commands and keep all his decrees, I will not bring on you any of the diseases I brought on the Egyptians, for I am the LORD, who heals you" (Exodus 15:26). God shows his faithfulness and love for the Israelites by protecting them from sickness and healing their diseases.

Tragically, however, the story line of Scripture shows us that Israel did not obey the covenant that God made with them (Exodus 19). Under the covenant at Sinai, God promised blessing for obedience and cursing for disobedience. A significant number of the curses that came from disobedience to God's law were related to sickness and disease. Ceremonial uncleanness to the law is also identified by leprosy, infection, and other sicknesses (Leviticus 13–14). Moses lists the consequences of disobedience to the law in Deuteronomy 28—diseases, wasting disease, fever, boils, tumors, festering sores, madness, blindness, hunger, thirst, severe and lingering illnesses, and plagues. All of these curses would fall on God's people for failing to obey all of his commands and decrees (Deuteronomy 28:15). These examples were given to reveal God's use of sickness and disease as judgment, as well as to point to his power to heal when the people returned to him in repentance and cried out for healing and deliverance.

Visit the Sick

We see God showing mercy, for example, in healing Miriam from leprosy after she had been afflicted with the disease for her disobedience (Numbers 12:9–15). We see that Miriam's healing came about because of Aaron's burden and concern as he pleads with Moses to ask God for mercy on her behalf. God shows compassion and care, honoring Aaron's heartfelt request and showing his compassionate heart toward Miriam by healing her in her affliction.

God's use of sickness and disease in both judgment and healing continues as Israel enters the Promised Land and human kings are established to rule over them. King David's son becomes sick and dies because of David's adultery (2 Samuel 12:14–18). King Asa becomes diseased in his feet, and though his disease is severe, he wrongly seeks physicians *instead* of the Lord and dies as a result (2 Chronicles 16:12–13). Despite these signs of judgment, we also see God's powerful hand of healing. God heals King Hezekiah, who was mortally ill and had been told he would die (2 Kings 20:1–11). God brings healing to a little boy through Elijah as a result of the mother's plea to the Lord (1 Kings 17:17–24). Though God brings sickness on people as judgment for their disobedience, God also shows his kindness to many by healing them.

The clear picture that develops through the story line of Scripture is that even though sickness and disease are signs of judgment and evidence of the curse, God brings relief and hope from the curse as well. During Israel's time of exile, the prophets bring hope of redemption through the figurative use of sickness/healing. The prophet Jeremiah speaks of the heart that is "beyond cure" (Jeremiah 17:9), yet it is the Lord who is our hope (Jeremiah 17:13), who will heal and save (Jeremiah 17:14). The prophet Isaiah inspires hope in the Redeemer, the Messiah, who is to be pierced for our transgressions, crushed for our iniquities, and wounded for our healing (Isaiah 53:5). These references to the healing of sickness from the prophets ultimately describe God's saving work and his forgiveness of sins. The psalmist writes of his hope in God, the one who forgives all our sins and heals all our diseases (Psalm 103:3). The prophets point to redemption by means of a spiritual healing by a sovereign God who heals and saves from spiritual sickness through the coming Messiah.

God's unfolding story line of redemption also reveals his call on his people to care for those who suffer from sickness and disease. God, through the prophet Ezekiel, chastises the shepherds of Israel for neglecting their flock. Though the leaders of Israel were neglecting the people of God in several ways, one in particular was failing to care for the sick. Ezekiel writes, "You have not strengthened the weak or healed the sick or bound up the injured. You have not brought back the strays or searched for the lost. You have ruled them harshly and brutally" (Ezekiel 34:4). Ezekiel's concern was that the shepherds' neglect in caring for the sick would lead the people to neglect them as well.

Throughout Israel's history, we see that God had a divine design to use sickness, disease, and affliction to achieve his purposes. The Old Testament ends with the prophets declaring that though God's people are scattered, disobedient, and discouraged, they should continue to wait in hope for the promised redeemer and healer. Despite a tragic history of God's people living in disobedience, God is faithful to the covenant he made with his people. The time will come when he will send a redeemer who will usher in the long-awaited kingdom of God.

The Life of Christ

After many years of silence, God eventually broke through the despair and suffering with a voice calling in the wilderness to prepare the way for the Lord (Mark 1:3). The voice belonged to a man named John the Baptist, and he was the forerunner who would prepare others for the coming of the Redeemer. All four gospels identify Jesus as this Redeemer, the long-awaited Messiah who was to save his people from their sins and usher in the kingdom of God. Mark points us to Jesus Christ as the Redeemer in Jesus' first recorded words in Mark's account: "The time has come," he said. "The kingdom of God has come near. Repent and believe the good news!" (Mark 1:15). Jesus brings the kingdom of God near, making it accessible to rebellious, disobedient people.

Mark's account of the good news about Jesus gives evidence that Jesus came in the authority of God as the Son of God (Mark 1:1). One of the primary evidences is his authority over sickness, disease, and death. In fact, all of the gospel writers remind the reader of this reality in what becomes a constant summary pattern: "News about [Jesus] spread all over Syria, and people brought to him all who were ill with various diseases, those suffering severe pain, the demon-possessed, those having seizures, and the paralyzed; and he healed them" (Matthew 4:24). Time after time, we see Jesus healing people, fulfilling the words of the prophet.

God's Care for the Sick

We see this in John's gospel as well when he writes of a blind man from birth who encounters Jesus (John 9:1–7). In verse 2, the disciples ask a question that assumes the common understanding of God's purposes in sickness—that sickness is the result of God's judgment on sin: "Rabbi, who sinned, this man or his parents, that he was born blind?" Jesus' response indicates that there is a transition under way from Israel's bondage to the coming kingdom in which Jesus is King: "Neither this man nor his parents sinned," said Jesus, "but this happened so that the works of God might be displayed in him" (verse 3). John points to a purpose beyond the healing, to the display of God's work of redemption through the work of his Son.

The authority of Jesus and the coming kingdom are most clearly seen, however, when Jesus raises the dead. Jesus revives the synagogue leader's little girl who had died (Mark 5:41–42). He raises Lazarus from the dead after his body has been lying for several days in the tomb (John 11:44). Ultimately, these actions point to his own physical resurrection from the dead three days after dying on the cross. In the Messiah's own resurrection, his followers are not only promised eternal life through repentance and faith in him; they are promised a physical resurrection on the final day: "For if we have been united with him in a death like his, we will certainly also be united with him in a resurrection like his" (Romans 6:5). In the resurrection of Jesus, we see confirmation of the promise of our own resurrection and the ultimate defeat of the curse of sin, sickness, and death.

God's sovereign power over sickness and disease in Jesus' authority is undeniable throughout the gospel accounts, but we must not miss the call that Jesus gives to his followers to *care for* those who are afflicted. The clearest example is in Matthew 25, where Jesus teaches his disciples a parable about kingdom living in caring for others in his name: "For I was hungry and you gave me something to eat, I was thirsty and you gave me something to drink, I was a stranger and you invited me in, I needed clothes and you clothed me, I was sick and you looked after me, I was in prison and you came to visit me" (Matthew 25:35–36). Jesus powerfully teaches that in those moments when the disciples care for their least brother, they are also offering care to the King (verse 40). Here we see that Jesus closely identifies himself with his suffering people. He ends his teaching by warning that judgment will fall on the wicked—those who do not care for him by neglecting to care for others (verses 41–46).

In the Gospels, we learn that Jesus ushers in the kingdom of God, and a primary evidence that redemption has come is that the blind receive sight, the lame walk, the deaf hear, the sick and diseased are healed, and the dead are raised. We also learn from the teaching of Jesus that God has designed his people to care for one another as a powerful representation of his compassion for the weak and needy. And as the story continues to unfold in the birth and life of Christ's church, we see further evidences that the kingdom of God has arrived in the person of Jesus as his followers await the fulfillment of God's promises in his future return.

The Life of the Church

When Jesus sent out his disciples, he commanded them to "heal the sick, raise the dead, cleanse those who have leprosy, drive out demons" (Matthew 10:8). This work continues as the church is birthed at Pentecost (Acts 2) and as the apostles go out to be Christ's witnesses to the world (Acts 1:8). In the story of the apostles and the early church we again see God's sovereign power to judge, as well as to heal. Ananias and Sapphira receive divine judgment in death because they pretended to give the full portion of the proceeds from their sold property to the apostles (Acts 5:1–11). God also shows his hand of healing as a measure of compassion on Tabitha and on those who loved her; after Tabitha fell sick and died, Peter raised her from the dead (Acts 9:36–43).

In the letters of the apostles we gain further insight into God's sovereign redemptive purposes in sickness and suffering. Paul refers to "a thorn" in his flesh that was given to him so the power of Christ would be powerfully displayed in his weakness (2 Corinthians 12:8–9). Sickness and death were used by God as a means to warn the church against abusing the Lord's Table (1 Corinthians 11:30). Peter urged Christians who suffer according to the will of God to see their suffering as an opportunity to commit their souls to their faithful Creator (1 Peter 4:19). Throughout the story of the early church we see God using sickness, pain, disease, and suffering as a way of sanctifying his kingdom people and magnifying the worth of Christ.

Just as clearly, however, there is a call for those in the church to care sacrificially for the afflicted in order to achieve these redemptive purposes. A powerful example is found in the book of Acts when several Christians sell their properties and lay the proceeds at the apostles' feet to be used to serve those in need (Acts 4:34–37). Paul refers to the sickness of Epaphroditus as he writes to the church in Philippi, and the care and concern of Paul and the church for this man are evident (Philippians 2:25–27). James exhorts Christians to call on the elders to pray for the sick (James 5:14). John prays for the Christians: "I pray that you may enjoy good health and that all may go well with you, even as your soul is getting along well" (3 John 2).

In these examples there is evidence that the early followers of Christ showed sympathy for the sick and needy and felt called to sacrificial action by serving those in need. We find a confidence in the face of sickness that God's sovereign design can be accomplished through it. Both individual Christians and local church bodies are called to care for those in the church who are sick, hurting, afflicted, and suffering until Jesus returns for his church and consummates his kingdom.

New Creation

At some point in the future, the unfolding of God's redemptive plan for creation will come to fulfillment. That final destination for those who follow Christ is not a disembodied existence of life after death. When Jesus returns, he will come for his bride, judge the nations, punish the wicked, and fully consummate his kingdom in the new heaven and new earth. This state is commonly referred to as the new creation—a time when the curse of sin is fully and permanently reversed. God's kingdom people will not just experience physical resurrection from the dead; they will enjoy eternal fellowship with Jesus in a world free from sin, sickness, and death.

A wonderful hope is that we will have physically whole bodies that are not cursed. In Revelation, John paints a vivid picture of a world in which sickness, disease, pain, suffering, affliction, and death are no more: God "will wipe every tear from their eyes. There will be no more death or mourning or crying or pain, for the old order of things has passed away" (Revelation 21:4). Reminiscent of the Garden of Eden where the first humans lived (Genesis 2), John speaks of a centrally located river and a tree of life whose leaves are for the healing of the nations (Revelation 22:1–2). This is an indication that the curse has been reversed and those who belong to the kingdom of God through the cross of Christ will experience what God intended in the Garden of Eden.

Understanding the unfolding story line of the Bible is essential if we are to grasp God's design and plan for his creation, and it is necessary to comprehend God's eternal purposes for sickness, disease, pain, and affliction in our world. Despite the sickness or affliction that someone in our church may be currently experiencing, we have the glorious privilege of pointing them to a greater, divine, and more significant reality than the pain of their physical circumstances. We can remind them that sickness and affliction are results of the fall and that our dying bodies are reminders of our birth into sin. Some may need reminders that sickness was a means for God to discipline his chosen people and to teach them to long for a redeemer. We can rejoice in the healings and restorations that are signs of the coming of God's kingdom and the authority of the Son of God, given to us as a foretaste of what we will fully experience when Jesus returns and resurrection becomes a reality.

The Bible's teaching on sickness and disease should also move us to respond in worship to our great, eternal, and sovereign God who controls sickness and healing in his infinite wisdom for the good of his people and his own glory. We should respond with a great passion to care for those who are sick, afflicted, and needy in light of the biblical responsibility set before us as followers of Christ. May these considerations of biblical truth prepare you, not only for your own afflictions (that are certain to come), but as you sacrificially care for people in your church—people who long to experience the fellowship of Jesus in their affliction. Know that as you do this you fulfill the words of Christ: "'When did we see you sick or in prison and go to visit you?' The King will reply, 'Truly I tell you, whatever you did for one of the least of these brothers and sisters of mine, you did for me'" (Matthew 25:39–40). May we be faithful to do likewise!

CHAPTER 2

SPIRITUAL CARE FOR THE SICK

Theological Precision

> I venture to say that the greatest earthly blessing that God can give to any of us is health, *with the exception of sickness.*
>
> Charles Spurgeon, *An All-Round Ministry*

DOCTRINE LAYS THE FOUNDATION for application. The apostle Paul models this pattern in his New Testament letters. Many of the great Christian preachers of history have also borrowed this approach, and it is equally helpful to us in thinking about effective spiritual care of the sick. Though we can be effective in some practical ways and have some measure of wisdom pastorally, if our care is devoid of the hope of the gospel and the promises in God's word, the hope and encouragement we offer will be nothing more than an illusion.

Ask Leading Questions

You will need to be deliberate about your conversations when you visit the sick, and you should anticipate having to lead the interaction with the person you are seeing. The best way to prepare is to think about the types of questions that might eventually lead to a conversation beyond the day-to-day—to a spiritual conversation about the truth of the gospel and its promises. As you prepare, remember to whom you are talking. Most people who are sick or afflicted are, at the very least, uncomfortable. Some may also be dealing with intense pain, be in and out of consciousness, or be distracted by other family members in the room. Before we begin to ask questions, we should heed the wise counsel of David Dickson: "Don't let us strain them with anything requiring long or continuous attention, and let our change from one subject to another be natural and easy."[4] Give thoughtful consideration about what you should ask, and then proceed.

Here is a pattern that has been helpful for me to follow. I begin by asking the person about themselves and about their condition and the kind of treatment they are getting. Then I ask about their family, specifically about who has been caring for them during this time. Then in some way I try to turn the conversation to topics of a spiritual nature. A helpful way to do this is to ask how you can pray for them. The Holy Spirit will often open an opportunity through this question and allow you to talk about eternal issues. Ask them how they are struggling. How are they relating to God through all of this? The most important theological question to ask, if appropriate, is, "Are you ready to die and stand before God?"[5] We ask questions so we can better learn about their situation and how they are handling it. This helps us to better know how to care for them both physically and spiritually. Good, thoughtful questions should lead us to talk about God and the hope we have—a hope that is only found in Christ. This is a hope we share together, both those who are sick and those who are healthy. Our questions should be sensitive to circumstances, but they should be God honoring and gospel driven in content.

Read Scripture

A young seminary student in my church decided to visit a dying church member in the hospital. He had very little experience with visitation, yet he heard me challenging our congregation to care for one of our longtime, faithful members who had taken a sudden turn for the worse. The student walked into her hospital room and found the woman in a disturbing state. She was semiconscious, gasping for every breath, and having seizures. He also found something quite unusual—there was no family in the room.

What would you have done in this situation?

Knowing there was nothing more to be done for her body and that the family was not around, he simply opened his Bible and began to read to her. As he stood over the bed of this dying woman gasping for breath, he read about the glorious character of God and his faithful promises to his adopted children in Christ. The woman passed away soon after this faithful brother left the room. In that moment, his instincts were sound. He knew that God's word is alive and active and sharper than any two-edged sword (Hebrews 4:12). Those who care for the sick must be prepared to have the truth of God's word on their lips to respond well when faced with difficult circumstances.

Visit the Sick

So how can we better prepare for these situations? I recommend meditating and studying through several Scriptures that may encourage the person you are going to see. It may be helpful to think through these passages in categories. Here are four categories I use, with a few suggested examples:

- **Passages of comfort:** Psalms 23; 28; 34; 46; 62; 145; Hebrews 4:14–16
- **Succinct gospel passages:** John 11:25–26; Romans 5:6–11; 2 Corinthians 5:17–21; Ephesians 2:1–10
- **Passages dealing with the purpose of suffering for the believer:** 2 Corinthians 12:7–9; James 1:2–4; 1 Peter 1:6–7; 4:12–19
- **Passages related to the reality and hope of eternity with Christ:** John 10:27–30; 14:1–3; Philippians 1:21–23; 1 Peter 1:3–5

Having a few passages memorized or on your mind when you visit will allow you to be better equipped for the unexpected. And in case you missed the obvious, make sure you bring your Bible with you!

Pray the Gospel

One morning, I received a call from a nurse at a local hospital asking me to come to the hospital as quickly as possible. The non-Christian spouse of one of our members was moments away from dying. I had no idea what I would find when I arrived. I walked into a room full of family members, with a heartbroken husband motioning me to stand beside his wife's bed. The husband was also suffering from some medical problems and had a tracheostomy that prevented him from speaking. It didn't take me long to see why I had been summoned. The man motioned to me to pray over his wife as the doctor removed her ventilator. Twenty minutes earlier, I had been in my office neck-deep in my studies. Now, I was being asked to pray a final prayer over a dying, non-Christian woman in front of her husband and fifteen to twenty non-Christian family members. I didn't have time to prepare, much less to think about, what I would say.

I decided to pray the gospel for this dying woman, her husband, and this room full of non-Christian family. I did not pray for God to spare her. I did not pray that God would heal her. I did not pray a manipulating request that God would receive her in her unrepentant state (which is what I think they expected me to pray). I prayed that the gospel was her only hope, and I prayed it in such a way that others in the room would leave with the clear understanding that the gospel was their only hope as well.

What do I mean by "praying the gospel"? Praying the gospel does not have to be complicated. It can be something as simple as this:

Father in heaven, as we are reminded at this moment of the fragility of life and the reality of our own mortality, we thank you that you remain righteous, just, and holy in all your ways as God and our Creator. We confess we have rebelled against your perfect word and character and deserve your just wrath and punishment because of our sins. Yet we thank you that you are rich in mercy and have provided a way for us to escape this judgment and be eternally reconciled to you. This hope is found only through your own Son's death on the cross in our place and his resurrection from the dead to give us new life. How great is your love that you would allow your perfect Son to die in the place of sinners by absorbing and satisfying your wrath so we could be made righteous before you. O God, thank you that this gracious offer of salvation comes, not by our own works, but by turning from our sins and trusting, by faith, in the person and work of Jesus. Father, may this be the hope and joy of us all, whether healthy or moments from death, so that you and your gospel would be known and glorified. In Jesus' name. Amen.

God taught me an invaluable lesson that day in the hospital room. When the gospel is prayed, the gospel is heard. Praying in the room that day, I longed for this dying woman to hear and receive Christ. In the moments before she faced judgment, my earnest hope was for her and her lost family members to hear the truth. If we truly believe that faith comes from hearing the message (Romans 10:17), we should never leave a hospital room, nursing home, rehabilitation center, or home of a sick person (or healthy person, for that matter) without praying the hope of God in Christ.

When you visit someone, make an effort to speak about God's righteousness, man's sinfulness, and Christ's death on the cross in our place for our sins. I realize that many circumstances can make this difficult to do. But nothing should prevent you from praying the gospel. Most people you visit will be open to receiving prayer, and it is a wonderful opportunity to speak truth to them before God and others in a way that feels natural. Remember that it is God alone through his Holy Spirit who transforms the darkest heart. Whether through prayer or proclamation, we should see every visit as a divine appointment to make known the saving power of the gospel.

Affirm the Promises and Attributes of God

God's promises, given to us through his word, expose our false hopes. But it is not merely knowing the promises of God that gives us hope; it is actually knowing and trusting the God who gave us these promises. Before you affirm the promises to someone, point them to the God of the promises. Use Scripture to bring to life the truth that the Lord is "righteous in all his ways and faithful in all he does" (Psalm 145:17). Remind them that God is sovereign over all things, including their affliction. Encourage them to know that God is omniscient (knows all things), omnipotent (all-powerful), omnipresent (everywhere), faithful, loving, and perfectly just, even as they suffer.

After lifting up and calling attention to the faithful, unchanging character of God, read to them the promises God makes to his chosen people in Christ. Read that nothing can separate them from the love of God that is in Christ Jesus (Romans 8:39). Remind them that God is their refuge and strength in distress (Psalm 59:16). Encourage them that their soul's hope is in God alone (Psalm 42:11). As we leave them, we want them to know more of God's character and promises, with these things on their minds and hearts, rather than leaving them with just our own wisdom and thoughts.

Trust God's Sovereign Plan

We must be deliberate and intentional in our care. Ultimately, though, we do the work of ministry knowing that we serve a sovereign God who is always working, and our peace must come from resting in that reality. Because God rules and controls all things, this theological consideration should lead to several expectations.

First, we should expect that *God is working through these situations*, regardless of the visible outcome. God can certainly use sickness and affliction to bring about salvation. God also uses sickness to mold and shape believers toward a heightened faithfulness when their health returns. Richard Baxter offers helpful instruction, suggesting the following as a way of nurturing an awakening: "If they recover, be sure to remind them of their promises and resolutions in time of sickness. Go to them purposely to set these home to their consciences; and whenever, afterwards, you see them remiss, go to them, and put them in mind of what they said when they were stretched on a sick-bed."[6] Often people forget the promises and commitments they make when they are facing sickness or affliction. As one caring for them, take time to remember these conversations and recall them at a later date. Whether sickness leads to salvation, recovery, or sweeter fellowship with Jesus until death, remind them to remember the ways they have seen God at work.

Second, we should expect that *God will use us*. Even though we can be insensitive, fumble our words, and have glaring weaknesses that can make us painfully ineffective, God is powerful and gracious, and he will use us to fulfill his purposes. One of these purposes is to mold and shape us toward greater trust in and dependence on him. The sovereignty and goodness of God is magnified when our own weakness and failure are made evident and we are ministered to by afflicted and suffering Christians. If God in his infinitely wise plan ministers to us through the sick, surely God can and will use us and our weaknesses to minister to them!

Third, we should expect that, by the power of the Holy Spirit, *God will give us the words to say*. D. A. Carson captures the common apprehension many feel as we worry about having the right words to say or as we wonder how to best pray for others:

> What, precisely, should we be praying for with respect to each member of our family—and why? Someone close to us contracts a terminal disease: what should we pray for, and why? For healing? For freedom from pain? For faith and perseverance? For acceptance of what has befallen? And would it make a difference if the person in question were seventy-five years of age, as opposed to twenty-nine? Why, or why not? Are there some things we may humbly request from God and others we should boldly claim? If so, what kinds of things fall into each category?[7]

These are certainly good questions to ask. At some point, however, we must trust in God's word treasured in our hearts (Psalm 119:11), our love for the individual whom we are visiting, and the sufficiency of the Holy Spirit as we depend on him for the words to say and to pray. Don't let your concern about having just the right words keep you from ministering God's power and grace to others in dependence on his Spirit.

Finally, we can expect that *God will use all these things for the joy of his people and the glory of his name*. What hope we have as Christians! Even in sickness and suffering, God will use our simple service for the joy and comfort of both the person who is sick and the one who visits. The driving purpose in all of this is God's glory. God is honored when the things of God are prayed. God is honored when his great character and ways are made known. God is honored when the sick and those caring for them have an unshakable faith and trust that he is working for their good and for his glory. Our aim must be God's aim—our joy in God, our love of God's people, and the glory of God's great name.

CHAPTER 3

WISE CARE FOR THE SICK

Pastoral Implications

> Even the stoutest sinners will hear us on their death-bed, though they scorned us before.
>
> Richard Baxter, *The Reformed Pastor*

A PASTOR IS REGULARLY FACED with unique challenges, issues, or situations that are not directly addressed in Scripture, yet which still require great wisdom and discernment. In moments like these, a pastor must learn to exercise *pastoral wisdom* as he makes choices that are empowered by the Holy Spirit, takes the related teaching of Scripture on an issue, and then acts in a manner that practically applies it to another situation. In other words, pastoral wisdom is the bridge that often unites biblical doctrine to an application in a new context or unique circumstance.

Another closely related bridge uniting doctrine and application is preaching. Here the pastor's task is to connect the truth of Scripture to the lives of his flock through application. The pastor's labor of study, prayer, and meditation on both

God's word and his people creates a bridge that unites doctrine and application together.

This work has both a theological and practical element to it. These "pastoral considerations" connect the theological (discussed in chapter 2) to the practical (what we will consider in chapter 4). These considerations deal with more than just surface issues; they reveal the heart, motive, and attitude behind our actions and thoughts.

Prepare Your Heart

Never underestimate the intuition of those who are sick. They can usually tell if we are visiting out of a sense of duty or obligation or out of genuine love. Before anything else, this is the first heart issue we must honestly assess. It's an easy trap to fall into, especially for pastors! We begin to think that visiting is just part of the job we've been hired to do. Pastors and paid staff must make a special effort to ensure they are visiting the sick out of love and care, not just out of a sense of obligation. Curtis Thomas, a seasoned American pastor of over forty years, writes: "Our visits should never appear only as professional duties. If the patient perceives that we are there only to carry out our responsibility, rather than having a genuine concern for him or her, our visit can do more harm than good."[8]

We also need to prepare our hearts for what we might see and experience. You may be visiting someone who is close to dying—and there are disturbing realities that accompany death. You may see blood or tubes and needles placed into unthinkable places. Deep pain, gasping for breath, and many other mannerisms can make even the toughest person squeamish. Yet these circumstances are not reasons to avoid caring for that person. In fact, these scenarios can be gifts that God gives to us that force us to prepare our hearts so we rely completely on the Holy Spirit for strength.

We must prepare our hearts, not just to avoid passing out, but so we are spiritually prepared as well. Before we come face-to-face with the person we are visiting, we should have in mind the Scriptures we want to read. We should think through the words of encouragement and hope we intend to bring. Whatever promises of God we choose to share, we should remind ourselves of them, believe them, and allow them to fill our hearts with joy. If we know and believe the truth we share with others, they are more likely to receive these words as truth from someone whose hope and confidence are evident as well.

Watch Your Time

How long should we stay when we visit someone? Does it differ, depending on whom and where we visit? A helpful starting place can be found in the wise words of Alistair Begg: "It is always better that people should feel our visit is too short than too long."[9] With this in mind, I recommend planning to stay no more than five to ten minutes in a hospital or nursing home setting. If the sick are in the hospital, you can safely assume they are experiencing some measure of pain. We actually care for them more faithfully by not pushing the line and staying too long. A home situation can be a little more flexible. Depending on the level of sickness and the pain of the individuals you are visiting, twenty to thirty minutes may be appropriate.

Visit the Sick

How soon should you visit after receiving word of an illness? This largely depends on the person's current condition and the nature of the affliction. In the nineteenth century, people often died from what we might consider "ordinary" illnesses. David Dickson, writing at that time, suggests, "When the elder does hear of such illness, he should visit *at once*. A day's, or even an hour's, unnecessary delay may cause him a long regret."[10] In the age of modern medicine, however, there is not the same sense of urgency there was a century or two ago. Still, there are certain emergencies that, once we receive word, should become our top priority. Like Dickson, if we delay and miss the passing of a dear brother or sister in Christ because of our procrastination, we will likely regret it and miss an opportunity to minister God's love and grace to someone in need.

Listen; Don't Solve

Being married is a wonderful gift from God that teaches us many things about ourselves and about men and women in general. One of the most noticeable is the striking difference in the ways that men and women deal with problems. Men typically want to take action, conquering and solving problems, while women want to be loved and nurtured. Since men are notorious for trying to solve problems, men who are ministering to sick persons need to remember that while problem solving can be a helpful gift, we must know when it is appropriate to utilize it and when we need to suppress the urge to fix things. Visiting the sick is one of those times when it is best to suppress this urge. In the discomfort of the moment, you may find yourself wanting to explain (with a thoughtful three-part thesis) to a precious soul lying in a hospital bed how God is going to use this affliction in his or her life. This is neither loving nor pastoral. Dickson gives a helpful alternative: "In cases of sudden and severe affliction, we may be able to do little more than weep with them that weep (Romans 12:15), giving that afflicted some word from the merciful and faithful High Priest, and perhaps taking hold of the sufferer's hand—an act of sympathy that often has a wonderful power to calm and soothe in times of deep distress."[11]

In other words, we need to simply listen and love. Fewer words can be more profitable in these scenarios than too many. Those suffering from affliction and sickness will feel more loved if we sympathize, not rationalize, with them in their illness. Listen; don't solve.

Leave a Note When Necessary

When I first started doing hospital visitations, I often found my efforts and time produced little in the way of results. This was not because the visits were bad; it was because I didn't even get to see the sick person! Sometimes they were sleeping or meeting with a team of doctors or out of the room for tests. I would leave and come back a few hours later, only to find they were unavailable again. I was wasting valuable time driving back and forth, and I found myself battling discouragement. How I wish someone had shared with me a simple and obvious tactic—leave a note.

There are countless reasons that a person may not be able to receive your visit. If they are in the hospital, they may be out of the room for a test. They may be unconscious or sedated.

They may be with a doctor or nurse and not taking visitors. In nursing homes, they may be participating in activities or sleeping. In rehab centers, patients regularly leave their room for therapy several times a day. When you visit someone at their home, they may be out at an appointment or even unable to get up and answer the door. Leaving a note is a simple way to communicate your care, and it accomplishes several things you would have done if you had been able to see them. Here is an example of a simple handwritten note I might leave for them:

> Dear _____,
>
> Sorry I [we] missed you. Know that I am praying for you and trusting God's sovereign plans and purposes for you in this difficult time. I talked with the nurse and will let the congregation know of your updated circumstances. Please let me know if there is any way I can serve you or your family through this time. You can reach me day or night at this number: _____.
>
> Grateful for you,
> Brian [and any others who may have been with you]

A note lets the person know you took the time to visit them, that you are praying for them, that you want to serve them, and that they are still connected to their local church in spite of their current circumstances. They can reread your note at any time to gain encouragement long after you have gone.

Enjoy the Moment

The stress and anxiety many experience in visiting the sick can sometimes cause them to miss the joy of this ministry. As you visit people, be mindful to enjoy all that God wants to accomplish for his glory. Here are a few opportunities in which you should anticipate God's providence.

1. See visiting the sick as a divine opportunity to care for those who may not care for you. Richard Baxter made this comment: "Even the stoutest sinners will hear us on their death-bed, though they scorned us before."[12] One of the hardest things to do is to love those who despise you, but this is exactly what our Savior commands us to do (Matthew 5:44; Luke 6:35). I recall that a struggling relationship I had with an elderly woman in our church greatly improved after I visited her at the hospital. Baxter's counsel is helpful in reminding us that obedience to Jesus is not optional. Enjoy seeing what God does when you are faithful to care for those who might not return the favor.

2. Caring for those who are hurting also increases your spiritual sensitivity. There is a unique joy in caring for people when they are most in need of care. This is a privilege that we only have while on earth. David Dickson writes about this privilege, "It is our part ... to do what [angels] are not privileged to do—to sit beside a dying believer, to smooth his pillow, to moisten his lips, to remind him of the rod and staff that are ready for his help in the dark valley [Psalm 23:4], and to direct his dying eye to Jesus. All this is a precious service we cannot render in heaven, but only on earth."[13] Caring for the sick and hurting is an honor that can bring great joy to us as Christians, if we are mindful to enjoy it.

3. In caring for the sick, we enjoy the gift of exercising our faith in Christ. There is no better place to experience the confidence of faith than alongside suffering saints who anticipate

meeting their Savior in a matter of moments. Christians' faith is magnified in suffering. Therefore, we should not only enjoy experiencing the gospel shining in suffering but also rejoice to be a witness of lives that end with rejoicing in the person and work of Christ as their only hope.

4. Finally, we need to enjoy how God molds, shapes, and teaches us through these experiences. This is one of the reasons I enjoy not just visiting the sick and dying but also performing funerals. Our hearts are wired to become so preoccupied with the affairs of life that we forget that death and sickness will one day fall on each of us. At any moment our lives can end. In caring for the sick and afflicted, we are reminded of the fragility of life and our closeness to eternity. We should enjoy these experiences that God gives us by his grace because they keep us mindful of the eternal—the things that are of lasting value.

Sitting at his father's bedside after watching him take his last breath, John Piper spoke these words:

> I look you in the face and promise you with all my heart: Never will I forsake your gospel. O how you believed in hell and heaven and Christ and cross and blood and righteousness and faith and salvation and the Holy Spirit and the life of holiness and love. I rededicate myself, Daddy, to serve your great and glorious Lord Jesus with all my heart and with all my strength. You have not lived in vain. Your life goes on in thousands. I am glad to be one.[14]

The pull of our culture today toward the comforts of life in this world demands that we as Christians do all we can to intentionally set our minds on the things above (Colossians 3:1–2). Visiting those who are sick and dying is one of the

means God gloriously uses to accomplish this h
in our lives. Embrace this aspect of God's grace

The truth is that you don't have to be a pastor to ﹏
pastorally. Pondering these kinds of considerations will help
you build a bridge from the theological convictions you have
about sickness, the sovereignty of God, and caring for those in
need so that you can minister to them.

CHAPTER 4

SKILLED CARE FOR THE SICK

Practical Necessities

> As long as we have a world wherein there is sin, it is a mercy that it is a world wherein there is sickness.
>
> J. C. Ryle, "Sickness"

WE MUST FIRST UNDERSTAND biblical doctrine in order to apply it properly and practically. However, the priority of doctrine should not diminish the need for practical skill in caring for the sick. We need a firm grasp of the practical issues to be effective. In fact, if we are not mindful of these practical considerations, we may end up failing to communicate the theological, which is where the hope of the gospel is found.

Make Eye Contact

We rarely think about the importance of looking someone in the eyes, that is, until we have a bad experience with someone. Think about a casual conversation. Looking them in the eyes communicates our interest in both the person and what they are saying. Bad eye contact—looking past them, glancing at our phone, looking down at the ground—all of this communicates disinterest, boredom, or preoccupation with other concerns. All of this is magnified when you are talking with someone in a hospital room. Good eye contact immediately communicates to someone that you are interested in them and that you are fully present and want to be there with them. Remember that the people you visit in a hospital or nursing home are likely to be sensitive about their appearance. They may have tubes coming out of them or machines pumping medication into them, and they aren't always prepared to receive visitors. Avoiding looking at them or having bad eye contact will only heighten their already sensitive disposition. So train yourself to look at them. Try to be disciplined with your eye contact.

Touch—with Discernment

Using physical touch to communicate care is something all of us must learn to do, not just those who are naturally touchy-feely persons. Appropriate physical touch lets a person know they are loved and cared for in ways that words cannot communicate. Many of those who are sick tend to develop "leprosy syndrome." In the first century, leprosy was a disease that led one to be banished from the city limits and become ostracized from their families and loved ones. Imagine what it would have felt like to be treated this way because of a physical disease. Though few today will develop actual leprosy, it can be common for sick persons, especially those in a hospital, to develop a sense that they are untouchable, someone to be avoided. One of the most effective ways to counter this tendency is through appropriate physical touch — touching a hand, arm, or foot when praying; giving a light hug; or physically helping a person move from a bed to a chair. These efforts can break down walls of insecurity and launch opportunities to build trust and deepen your ministry to them.

As you reach out to touch someone, be sure to use wisdom and discernment. Some people have a mixed response to physical touch. So be aware of this and make sure you pay attention to what the person says in response and how they react to your touch. Also keep in mind that appropriate touch will vary, depending on the age, gender, and type of relationship you have with a person. For example, as a middle-aged man I am very comfortable holding the hand of an eighty-five-year-old widow whom I know very well. This woman likely sees me as someone like a grandson to her. I would not be as comfortable, however, physically touching a female church member who is closer to my own age (whether married or single). Physical touch can be amazingly effective, but discernment is needed. So be wise with how you use it.

Be Pleasant

My eighty-year-old grandmother loves NBA basketball, and she once told me her favorite basketball player was Dennis Rodman. If you don't know who Dennis Rodman is, he had a reputation for being one of the worst "bad boys" in the history of sports. Needless to say, I was not only surprised but a bit concerned, wondering why my grandmother would pick him as her favorite player. So I asked why. In response, she said, "Because he smiles all the time." Still not sure what she meant, I cautiously questioned her again. "So he smiles a lot, Grandma?" "Yes," my grandmother answered back confidently, "and he *must* be having a good time. Why else would he be smiling so much?"

Though I still find it odd that Dennis Rodman was her favorite NBA player, this conversation reminded me of an important truth, one that is easily forgotten: *Don't forget to smile.* Smiling communicates something that words cannot. And people tend to like people who smile. So be pleasant. Look like you are enjoying yourself. Whether we like it or not, our demeanor affects how we are perceived. In fact, I have three specific recommendations about this:

1. Think about your facial expressions. While smiling helps, this is about more than just putting on a grin. In fact, you want to avoid putting on a facade. Instead, this is about self-awareness, about knowing yourself. We all have a natural "resting" face. It's the facial expression we make when we are relaxed. Some people, like me, by nature have a more serious expression. If this is true for you, you will need to work a little harder at cultivating a pleasant expression. The goal is to have a pleasant demeanor that communicates to the sick person that you are glad to be there.

2. Consider your posture — the way you stand and sit. You've probably heard that slouching during a job interview isn't going to earn you any points. And it is equally ineffective when you are visiting a sick person. Be aware of your posture and try to sit up in a way that lets the person know you are there to be present with them. You want them to feel like they have your undivided attention and respect.

3. Consider the tone of your voice. Your vocal tone and inflection can be a significant way of communicating warmth and care. On the other hand, a poor tone can sound harsh and insensitive. David Dickson again gives wise counsel: "A low, quiet voice is usually soothing and pleasant to them, especially if they are weak and nervous. Don't let us strain them with anything requiring long or continuous attention."[15] This principle is proven true if you've ever spent time around babies. Infants, even before they understand a word we say, are impacted by the tone of our voice. A loud and abrupt voice scares an infant, while a gentle and soothing voice produces smiles and coos. Obviously, this isn't an exact science. We simply need to realize that our face, voice, and other physical expressions powerfully communicate long before one truth is uttered from our mouth.

Be Perceptive

Regardless of where our visit takes place, we must be aware of our surroundings. In a hospital room, a sick person will be lying in a bed, and we'll also typically see IV lines, machine cords, oxygen lines, call buttons, blood pressure cuffs, and, occasionally, a roommate. All of this changes the environment and the nature of the interaction with the sick individual. You may find other family members or doctors present. When you first enter the room, take note of your surroundings, be mindful of these issues, and make visual notes to yourself as you prepare for your visit.

In addition, take note of your position relative to the person when you are speaking to them. If possible, speak to them at the same level. Instead of standing over them as they lie in bed, pull up a chair and position yourself at eye level. This may seem like a minor detail, but it puts others at ease and makes the visit less threatening. Take note of any indications that the person is in pain. This will be easier if you have planned ahead and know something of their condition. In hospital settings, it is not difficult to find out this information.* While we certainly cannot know all that is going on with the people we are visiting, a little homework and some awareness of our surroundings can make a vast difference in the comfort level of our visit.

Freshen Your Breath

Can you recall how you felt the last time you spoke with someone whose breath took your breath away (and not in a good way)? Consider how distracting and unpleasant it was. What was your impression of that person after that encounter? Bad breath can be a touchy subject, and some can be offended or embarrassed if you bring it to their attention. It makes any conversation awkward and uncomfortable. However, here is a simple solution for everyone. Be humble and aware, and plan ahead. Always carry gum or mints with you to take care of potential problems. There are many things that can negatively affect your ministry to others, but this is one that can easily be eliminated with a little awareness and planning.

That said, be sure you are gracious toward the person you are visiting. Even though you are thinking ahead about this, it is an unrealistic expectation for sick people, who typically haven't showered or brushed their teeth in days. In many cases,

---

* For further details, see appendix 3, question 7.

there is little they can do about this problem, and they may be especially self-conscious about their appearance. Therefore, be gracious and sensitive to their situation.

These are just a few practical issues to consider when visiting the sick. As you plan and prepare for a fruitful visit with someone, keep in mind that God causes the growth and is ultimately responsible for the outcome (1 Corinthians 3:7). Be practical, but depend on God's grace and his Holy Spirit! We must not be deceived into thinking that our own ability exercised in our own power can produce spiritual fruit, lest we conduct our visits with prideful and self-sufficient hearts. I offer these suggestions and encourage awareness of these practical issues so you can be even more effective in breaking down barriers to a fruitful ministry visit.

COMMUNITY CARE FOR THE SICK

Equipping the Saints

PASTORS, WHILE YOU MAY be the person primarily responsible for visiting the sick in your congregation, this book is *not* just for you. Though I wrote this with pastors in mind, my hope is that it will also be used to train and equip congregation members in this task as well. I pray that you will be challenged to visit the sick and also that you will be convicted of the importance of training your people to do likewise. With this goal in mind, I commend to you five ways in which you can effectively teach, train, and motivate your people to see the value in caring for the afflicted and dying within your church.

Exhort through Preaching

As you preach the Bible, look for points of application that serve as exhortations to love, care, and serve the sick and afflicted in your church. Refer to the chapter on biblical considerations for some examples of relevant passages. Regardless of the Bible passage you are preaching, I am confident you will find an expression there of a sovereign God who is ruling over the affliction and suffering of people. You will see God's glory displayed in his people who care for those in need for the sake of the gospel. This is one reason that expositional preaching is a helpful, steady diet for a local church. As you preach through the various books of the Bible, you are more likely to be confronted with texts that lend themselves to this type of instruction. That said, there is nothing wrong with doing a short sermon series on this topic when it seems appropriate. Regardless of *how* you teach your congregation to visit the sick—whether through a short sermon series or through regular application in your expositional sermons—never forget that the preaching of God's word is what gives life to the church, and it is the setting for us to exhort with authority the matters that are most important to the spiritual health of the entire body. Teach your church that the care of the sick and afflicted is a priority for God's people by exhorting them through public preaching.

Pray for the Afflicted in Public Gatherings

I will be the first to admit that praying for a seemingly never-ending list of health needs each week can easily turn into the mouthing of meaningless, painful mantras. So drop that from your mind; it's not what I'm proposing here. Instead, I encourage you to pick a couple of significant afflictions in your church to highlight through public prayer for the purpose of informing and teaching your congregation how we as Christians should face these common struggles. Praying for these serious situations lets the congregation know about what is going on with specific individuals and also allows you an opportunity to teach your congregation how to face these difficulties.

When you pray, be sure to pray *specific* biblical truths. Praise God for his sovereign power over sickness and death. Thank God for the hope we have of physical wholeness and resurrection one day because of Christ. Pray for healing if it is God's will to heal. Pray for the gospel to be known in the lives of those who are suffering as Christ is magnified in our weakness. Pray for the medical personnel caring for them, while recognizing God as the great healer. Then pray that as a local church the gospel will be seen in our faithful care of those enduring affliction. Utilize the public gatherings of the church to pray for these needs — they provide wonderful moments to teach and motivate and demonstrate that there is great power in corporate intercession.

Inform Your People Regularly

Church members are more likely to serve the sick and afflicted if they know what is going on and where to go. Lack of knowledge can be discouraging for someone who wants to help but doesn't know how to gather the appropriate information. Create a system that regularly informs church members of needs within the church and updates them as circumstances develop and change. In the past, bulletins and prayer chains have been used effectively to communicate this information, and they can still be quite useful today. Church-wide e-mail lists, the church website, and social media can also be ways to communicate this information to people. Whatever the method, be committed to keeping your people updated on the circumstances (so they know how to pray better) and to get them information about how to visit and care for those who are struggling. Pass along the name of the hospital, the room number, whether the person wants visitors, how close someone might be to dying, and suggestions for things that church members can do for those in need. These are just a few specific details that are helpful for people to know. Remember, most of the people in your church aren't used to the regular patterns and habits of pastoral labor. Busy church members can easily find reasons not to bother with caring for the sick. Don't let lack of information be one of those reasons!

Lead by Example

We cannot expect our people to be faithful in this task if we are not fully engaged and committed. We can preach about caring for the sick; we can pray in every public gathering for them; we can give a detailed assessment of the daily needs of the afflicted. But if we are not personally engaged in visiting the sick ourselves, we have failed. A soldier who is willing to follow a general into battle may have reservations when asked to lead the charge while the leaders command from a distant post, far from the front lines. Fellow pastors, make it your priority not just to visit but to model an obvious passion for the sick and afflicted. People will look to you for an example of ministering with faith in our sovereign God and of a tender fellowship with our Savior. May your words and actions communicate the truth that God works all things for his own glory and the good of his people. Lead faithfully in this way, and your people will follow.

Lift Up the Example of Others

As important as it is for you to be a model to others, you don't need to be the only one engaged in this ministry. Seize key opportunities to praise and lift up laypeople in your church who faithfully care for the afflicted and dying. Each Wednesday at our church, we take the time to informally share what we are thankful for. I will often use this time to highlight a faithful brother or sister who sacrificially cared for a dying member that week and will give thanks for their effort and faithfulness. As you lift up those who are faithful to visit the afflicted, God will use that example as a way to move others to do the same.

My fellow colaborers in the gospel, this is a short book written for a simple but essential purpose: to emphasize the biblical importance of visiting and caring for the sick. I hope it will aid you in faithfully shepherding your flock. And I hope it proves useful in teaching and equipping your flock to care for one other. May God use the calling he has given to us, not just to urge others to care for the sick, but to use all our labors for his good purposes and the glory of his great name.

CONCLUSION

> During that epidemic of cholera, though
> I had many engagements in the country, I
> gave them up that I might remain in Lon-
> don to visit the sick and the dying.
>
> Charles Spurgeon, *C. H. Spurgeon's*
> *Autobiography*

CHARLES SPURGEON IS OFTEN CELEBRATED as one of Christianity's most gifted, dedicated, and brilliant preachers and pastors. He is often praised for his piercing, articulate, Christ-centered, and word-driven sermons, messages that were either heard or read by thousands of people all over the world. Because Spurgeon was renowned for his preaching and speaking, it is easy to overlook another aspect of his ministry—his faithfulness in caring for his congregation in sickness and crisis.

In 1854, at the young age of twenty, Spurgeon became pastor of a church in London (New Park Street Chapel), which later became the Metropolitan Tabernacle. Spurgeon had barely been in London twelve months when a severe case of cholera swept through London. Spurgeon recounts his efforts to care for and visit the numerous sick in the midst of horrific conditions: "All day, and sometimes all night long, I went about from house to house and saw men and women dying, and, oh, how glad they were to see my face! When many were afraid to enter their houses lest they should catch the deadly disease, we who had no fear about such things found ourselves most gladly listened to when we spoke of Christ and of things Divine."[16]

Here we have an example of a young, inexperienced pastor who feared God more than a contagious disease. Spurgeon is a model for each of us of what it looks like to sacrificially care for others, even at great risk to ourselves. Spurgeon did this because he knew there was rare spiritual fruit that could only ripen at the bedside of a dying man.

Spurgeon made visiting the afflicted a priority in his life and ministry. Even as a young pastor, Spurgeon's gift to preach was evident to all who heard him, which brought great demand on his time. Yet Spurgeon would often turn aside from these opportunities to care for the needs of people. He recounts, "During that epidemic of cholera, though I had many engagements in the country, I gave them up that I might remain in London to visit the sick and the dying."[17] Even at twenty years of age, the demands on his time were great, possibly greater than the demands most of us face who pastor today. In Spurgeon's example we can see the importance he placed on visiting the sick, and he emphasizes that this priority is not just for pastors and leaders in the church—it is for all "who love souls."[18]

That's what care for the sick ultimately reveals—our deep love for souls, specifically the souls of those with whom we have made a covenant in our local church. As we fellowship, love, care, and encourage one another, let us not lose sight of those who can all too easily be forgotten. Those who are sick don't have the energy or the ability to fight for our attention, like so many other things in our lives do. Instead, we must take the initiative. Visiting the sick will not slide easily into our schedules. It will interrupt our plans. But we must not grow discouraged or frustrated. We must take heart. As we are intentional in our calling to visit the sick, we can trust that we are engaged in a divine task — souls are being loved and nurtured; we ourselves are being transformed into the likeness of Jesus Christ; the gospel is being revealed through this ministry; and God is being glorified.

AFTERWORD

WELL, THERE YOU HAVE IT—a practical manual on how to visit the sick. Brian has given us a number of instructive concepts to consider. But unless the rubber meets the road, all of this effort is nothing more than intellectual gymnastics. So here are my questions to you: Are you willing to stick your neck out and do it? Are you willing to risk your comfort to care for those in need?

Let me illustrate why it is better to risk rejection than to play it safe. It comes from the world of medicine, the world in which I live and work each day. If a surgeon ever tells you he has *never* taken out a normal, healthy appendix, you will want to think twice before using his services. Why? Because the task of diagnosing appendicitis is not all that exact. A good surgeon will do his best but will occasionally miss. So if you meet a surgeon who has never taken out a normal appendix, the truth is that he has probably missed a few cases over the years. In other words, *for a person to be healed, a doctor needs to take the risk.*

Likewise, when you visit a sick person, you must take a risk. You will need to risk delving into the uncertain waters of a gospel presentation. Yes, you may get shot down in your efforts, but if you never risk your comfort or pride in sharing this news, you will never see the healing power of the gospel either. Like a surgeon who sometimes takes out a normal appendix, your efforts may not always go as you hope they will; yet in the end, it is far better to have a bruised ego than to be disobedient to our Lord's command to share the gospel and comfort the sick. So take the risk and share the good news. You won't regret it.

Brian has given us useful tools in this book, and I encourage you to use them. The proverbial ball is now in your court.

A very blessed dad,

William V. Croft, MD

ACKNOWLEDGMENTS

A SPECIAL THANKS TO—

The many faithful laborers who read over this manuscript and gave helpful input. Your comments and counsel were of immense value. I want to especially acknowledge the tireless labors of Scott, Adam, Greg, and Matt, whose time and gifts toward this project I could never repay.

The good folks at Zondervan and their partnership in not just this book but this series. Thank you for believing enough in this book that you would republish it and trust it to still be a useful tool for pastors.

The faithful saints of Auburndale Baptist Church, who allow me the gift of your fellowship, the encouragement of your love, and the endless support of my labor in the word for the sake of your souls. I gain great joy from watching God further the gospel and build his church through your desire, submission, and worship of him.

Mark Dever, not only for writing the foreword but for the invaluable investment, teaching, instruction, and guidance you have given me through the years.

Don Whitney, for your wisdom, counsel, and guidance throughout the writing of this book. Learning from you in this way has been a precious gift.

My father, for your endless encouragement in this project and for your powerful and selfless example to me my whole life of what it means to care for not just the physical needs but also the spiritual needs of others.

My children—Samuel, Abby, Isabelle, and Claire. What unspeakable joy you bring me by your love, care, and affection! You remain a daily example to me of God's undeserved goodness and grace.

My wife, who remains the most compelling example of the topic of this book by your unconditional care of me. Apart from my Savior, there is no one I love more than you.

Our sovereign, eternal God and King Jesus, who forgives all our sins, heals all our diseases (Psalm 103:3), and in his infinite wisdom and mystery displays himself most powerfully in our weakness (2 Corinthians 12:9).

CHECKLIST

Visiting the Sick:
Theological, Pastoral,
and Practical Categories

Take this checklist with you and review it before visiting.

Theological

❑ Ask leading questions
❑ Read Scripture
❑ Pray the gospel
❑ Affirm the promises and attributes of God
❑ Trust God's sovereign plan

Pastoral

❑ Prepare your heart
❑ Watch your time
❑ Listen; don't solve
❑ Leave a note when necessary
❑ Enjoy the moment

Practical

❑ Make eye contact
❑ Touch with discernment
❑ Be pleasant
❑ Be perceptive
❑ Freshen your breath

SPIRITUAL CONVERSATIONS

Pastor-Patient Conversation

This is an example of a conversation inside a hospital room between a pastor and patient that moves from small talk and physical issues to a spiritual conversation.*

Please realize this is one of many possible scenarios, depending on the answers given by the individual. I pray this example will encourage you to see the value of thinking about these prospective opportunities before you find yourself in them.

Pastor: I have been enjoying our conversation, but can I put you on the spot and ask you a personal question?

Patient: Uh, yeah, I guess so.

Pastor: In light of your physical condition, have you considered what happens to each of us when we die?

Patient: Yes, I have begun to think about that more and more.

Pastor: Are you ready to die and stand before God?

Patient: I don't know. I hope so.

---

* A helpful resource for thinking more deeply about this issue is Don Whitney, "Ten Questions to Ask to Turn a Conversation Toward the Gospel," http://biblicalspirituality.org/wp-content/uploads/2011/02/Ten-questions-to-ask.pdf (accessed October 21, 2013).

Pastor: Why do you believe God would allow you into heaven?

Patient: I've lived a pretty good life. I'm a good person.

Pastor: Are you interested in hearing what the Bible says about this?

Patient: Yes, I think I would like to know.

Pastor: The Bible teaches that God is eternally holy, righteous, and perfect in all his ways (Psalm 145). God created the world, and it was good and perfect, including man, who was made in God's image (Genesis 1–2). Yet when Adam and Eve sinned and rebelled against God's commands, they brought sin into the world, which eternally separated them from God (Genesis 3). The consequence of sin in the world is that we as Adam's descendents are now born into sin and are thus guilty of rebellion against God (Romans 5:12). Another consequence of this sinfulness is that God in his holy and righteous character must punish sin by death (Romans 6:23), and as a result we are described as deserving of his wrath and judgment (Ephesians 2:3).

However, the Bible also teaches that God is rich in mercy (Ephesians 2:4) and, in his amazing love for sinners, provided a way for us to not only escape his judgment but be eternally reconciled back to God (2 Corinthians 5:18). All this was accomplished by his own Son, Jesus, who was born a human just like us (Philippians 2:8). Although he lived a perfect, sinless life, he died on the cross. On the cross, God accomplished his reconciling purpose as his own Son bore the full wrath and judgment of God in our place (2 Corinthians 5:21). He rose from the dead three days later, conquering death and providing us life through him (Romans 4:25). Through Jesus, we not only have forgiveness of our sins (Colossians 1:14), but we also have his righteousness given to us so we can stand blameless before God (2 Corinthians 5:21). We receive this, not by anything we have done, but through faith in who Jesus is and the work he accomplished on the cross, shedding his own blood on our behalf (Romans 5:8 – 10). We must simply acknowledge our sin and rebellion against God, see that Jesus is the one who sufficiently paid our penalty for sin (Hebrews 10:12), repent (turn) from our sins, and by faith alone trust in Jesus (Mark 1:15). Have you ever heard this before? How does this strike you?

Patient: Well, I would like to think about what you have shared with me. Is there a way I can reach you if I have more questions?

Pastor: Sure. [Give mobile phone number.] Know that this is a very appropriate time in your life to consider these issues seriously. Do you mind if I pray with you?

Patient: No, I would like that.

Doctor-Patient Conversation

This is a more conversational example of how my father, a Christian physician who has practiced medicine for over thirty years, typically seeks to accomplish this same objective.

Doctor: John, can I put you on the spot?

Patient: I guess so.

Doctor: All of us will face death at some time. But your condition will require you to look at death sooner than some. When you die, do you think you will go to heaven?

Patient: I think so [or hope so]. (If this response is given, you know the patient either cannot verbalize the gospel or does not know it.)

Doctor: John, when you stand before the Lord and he says, "John, why should I let you into heaven?" — what would your response be?

Patient: Well, I've been a good person.

Doctor: John, let me give you a few issues to consider. If I were to ask you the characteristics of God, you would probably tell me that God is loving, holy, all-knowing, all-powerful, kind, and so forth. But the characteristic that gets you and me in trouble is that God is just.

Because of God's perfect justice, neither you nor I can spend eternity with a just and holy God if we have ever committed sin. There is an old saying that rings all too true: "Good people don't go to heaven; forgiven people go to heaven." God in his great mercy has made a way for sinners like you and me to be forgiven. When Christ came into the world, he had two main purposes — first, to show us a glimpse of who God is, and second, to provide a way for sinners to be reconciled to God and to be forgiven by him.

When Jesus died on the cross, he bore the punishment for the sins of anyone who would confess their state as a sinner and accept Jesus by faith alone as their Savior and Lord. He paid the price for our sin. At the moment we turn from sin and trust Christ, our sins are forgiven, and God sees us as though we have the righteousness of Christ. This is the great exchange—my sinfulness for his righteousness.

So the answer to the question about why the Lord should let you into heaven has nothing to do with what we do. It has everything to do with what Jesus did for us if we have accepted his offer of forgiveness. Has there ever been a time in your life when you confessed your sins and trusted in Jesus?

Patient: (One possible response) Yes, I have.

Doctor: Can you tell me about it? (Take it from here.)

Patient: (Another possible response) No, there has not.

Doctor: It is not my intention to coerce you into a decision. If you want, I will help you in the process of accepting Christ. If you would like to ponder these things further, you should feel free to do so.

(If you determine that the patient is a Christian, follow up as appropriate.)

Doctor: John, you've probably known all that I have told you but were just unable to verbalize these truths in a particular way. When I first asked you about going to heaven, you had an "I hope so" response. It is so very important for you as a Christian to know that you are guaranteed you will go to heaven when you die. That assurance will be a foundational truth you will want to hold on to as your condition progresses. Read the first eleven verses of Ephesians 1 and rest in the assurance that the Lord Jesus, through the apostle Paul, gives us. If you have any further questions, don't hesitate to contact me.

FAQ

THESE ARE FREQUENTLY ASKED QUESTIONS that are not addressed in the body of this work but are important issues that should be thoughtfully considered.

1. Is it a good idea for children to participate in visits?

When appropriate, include children in your visits to the sick. Children can lift the spirits of lonely, hurting persons in ways that our best efforts cannot. Their participation is also a wonderful way of training them to care for people. However, there are times when children should not accompany you on a visit—when a patient is in intense pain, is in a section of the hospital (such as the intensive care unit) where infections that are passed on can be harmful to the patient, or is a homebound person who is uncomfortable around children. These are just a few examples, but ultimately you will need to exercise wisdom and prayerful discernment in making a decision. When unsure, it is best to err on the safe side, knowing there will always be other opportunities to train and include your children in your labor.

2. Can playing musical instruments and singing be effective ways to care for the sick?

Yes, but only if you are gifted to do so. We don't want a sincere, well-meaning tone-deaf visitor bringing more misery on sick individuals. However, there are appropriate times to use music to lift spirits, soothe aches, and communicate biblical truth. It is important to proceed with sensitivity, based on the environment. Don't bring cymbals or play loudly in an emergency room, of course. But taking a group of people to a nursing home to sing Christmas carols at Christmastime is appropriate and deeply meaningful for singers and listeners alike.

3. How do I relate with other family members who are in the hospital room?

Always introduce yourself to everyone in the room and treat each of them with kindness and respect. If the patient is asleep or unconscious, others in the room can provide you with an update on the patient's condition. You may find opportunities to minister to the family and friends who are there. Still, we need to make sure that our main focus is on the patient. If you are talking with the family, make sure you keep your conversation relevant to the needs of the sick individual you came to visit.

4. What do I wear to visit someone who is in the hospital?

Use good judgment and common sense. Always take into consideration who you are visiting and what will be comfortable for them. Those from an older generation will probably expect you to be dressed more formally, while those of a younger generation will be comfortable with more casual attire. A safe middle ground is business casual. For men, this means shirts with button-down collars and dress pants or khakis (no jeans). For women, this typically means skirts or dresses that come to below the knee, or dress pants or khakis. Choose conservative shirts that are not too revealing. It is wise to be thoughtful about this issue, but don't obsess to the point of being more concerned about what you are wearing than about the care of the person you are visiting. Don't choose your wardrobe based on a fear of man.

5. At what time of day should most visits take place?

Try to honor the hospital's visiting hours if at all possible. When that isn't an option, determine how important is it that you pay a visit before another appropriate time would present itself. Although hospital patients sleep on and off throughout the day, avoid exceptionally early or late visits, which is a good general rule for hospitals and homes.

6. How do I lead into a spiritual conversation?

See appendix 2 for a couple of helpful examples of spiritual conversations.

7. How do I find a person's room in a hospital or nursing home?

You can generally call the hospital and request the patient's room number. Or, when you get to the hospital or nursing home, go to the information desk. The staff will give you the room number and give you the quickest and easiest route to the room. Hospitals can be overwhelming for some people, especially for those who aren't in them very often. Don't be embarrassed to ask for assistance. It is a way to cultivate humility and utilize the hospital's resources.

8. When is it appropriate to take someone with you?

Another way to ask the question is, "When *should* we take someone with us?" Here are a few great reasons: you need a second person for accountability reasons; you aren't comfortable going by yourself; you want to experience fellowship with another person; or you are ready to provide a training experience for another person. If you do take someone with you, take advantage of their observations of you in that environment and ask for feedback after the visit is over. The more intentional you are in evaluating your efforts, the more you will learn how to be effective in serving others.

9. How can I be respectful to the medical team caring for the people I visit?

It is tempting to bypass the nurses' station when coming to visit, especially if you already have the patient's updated information and room number or have been there previously. Remember that you reflect the gospel to those you encounter along the way, not just to the patient. Make a habit of stopping by the nurses' station, if for no other reason than to introduce yourself to the nurses who are caring for the person you have come to see. Ask how the patient is doing and if they have any updated information to share about their condition. Privacy laws typically prevent nurses from sharing much. However, by waiting patiently and speaking kindly to them, we affirm their authority and role in the care of the patient. This communicates respect, affirms them in their labor, and, most importantly, conveys a helpful picture of the gospel when we introduce ourselves as a pastor, deacon, or fellow church member of the patient.

10. How do I approach visiting someone who shares a room with another patient?

Though a semiprivate room is frequently seen as an inconvenience, it can also be seen as a great opportunity. We must remember to be polite, respectful, and sensitive so we do not disturb other patients when we come to visit. Nevertheless, always assume that the person in the other bed is attentive and listening to what you say when you visit. Whatever Scriptures, prayers, kind words, truths of the gospel, and hopeful promises of God you share with those you visit will also be heard by the other patient(s) in the room. The power of the Holy Spirit can reveal the truth of the gospel to him or her in the same way it can to the one you are visiting. As you leave, use pastoral wisdom to discern whether God has opened a door to minister to the other patient.

11. Should a pastor anoint with oil when praying for the sick?

This question is most often raised in light of James's instruction for "the elders of the church to pray over [the sick] and anoint them with oil in the name of the Lord" (James 5:14). Despite the fact that Scripture gives clear instruction on this matter, a debate remains among faithful pastors as to whether this practice should continue in today's church. Though people take many different positions on this issue, I believe the debate can be narrowed to two positions.

Medicinal Purposes: Some argue that in James's day anointing with oil was considered a medical means to aid the healing process, one that was to be accompanied by praying with faith for God to heal. Those who argue against anointing with oil today point out that oil is no longer used to treat sickness. A modern equivalent of this position would be to seek medical help while also praying in faith for God to heal according to his will.

Spiritual Purposes: This position argues for a New Testament connection with the Old Testament anointing of oil as a means of setting someone apart for God's blessing and Spirit to come. Those who adopt this position conclude that we should continue this practice today, anointing with oil as we ask God to show his favor on the sick and bring healing as the elders pray in faith. Proponents of this position may want to take a small bottle of oil with them on their visits for anointing and praying for the sick.

Determine first which position you feel is more accurate and binding to your conscience, and then decide if it would be valuable for you as a pastor to use anointing with oil along with your prayers for the sick.

12. What are some practical tools to use when visiting new parents in the hospital?

Yes, you read that correctly—I wrote "parents." What does visiting new parents have to do with visiting the sick? Pastors who serve in churches that have a majority of younger people may find there aren't many members who are dying. Yes, there will always be younger members who get sick, die from cancer, or die suddenly in a tragic accident. Some young children will die as well, but typically when a pastor is caring for the sick and dying in his congregation, it will most commonly be with those who are older.

Because of this, let me briefly address how to care for those you visit in the hospital after the birth of a new child. Pastors of churches with many young couples can stay very busy with fruitful visitation in hospitals if they visit the parents of every baby born into their congregation. In fact, if new babies are being born, I encourage you to celebrate these moments with the new parents. Here are ten practical tools to consider as you engage in ministry to parents of a new baby:

1. Be mindful of the stress and lack of sleep of new parents.
2. Be sensitive to the mother's recovery.
3. Introduce yourself to family in the room.
4. Wash your hands.
5. Hold the baby (if comfortable doing so).
6. Enjoy it!
7. Read Psalm 139:13–16.
8. Pray for the parents.
9. Plead for the soul of that child.
10. Keep an eye on how long you stay (typically less than twenty minutes).

This kind of ministry can be a great way to get your feet wet in going to hospitals, getting comfortable in them, and preparing for the more difficult hospital visits that every pastor is sure to encounter during his ministerial career.

"SICKNESS" (ABRIDGED VERSION)

J. C. Ryle

JOHN CHARLES RYLE is arguably the best-known and most influential Anglican bishop of the nineteenth century. Ryle is remembered for his uncompromising convictions, his faithful exposition of Scripture, his powerful Christ-centered preaching, his diligence in pastoral work, and his clarity in writing. Since his death on June 10, 1900, Ryle has continued to be a profound voice for the edification of the church and the furtherance of the gospel. In "Sickness", J. C. Ryle approaches the topic of illness in a biblically faithful, pastoral, and thoughtful manner. My hope is that in reading Ryle's heart on this matter, you will be led to a proper understanding of sickness and be fully equipped to care for the sick in your church to the glory of God.*

⁓

"The one you love is sick" (John 11:3).

---

* This essay on sickness written by J. C. Ryle has been abridged and minimally updated into the language of our day to increase its usefulness for modern readers. Scripture quotations are taken from the New International Version. This essay is in the public domain.

"Sickness" (Abridged Version)

The chapter from which this text is taken is well-known to all Bible readers. In lifelike description, in touching interest, in sublime simplicity, there is no writing in existence that will bear comparison with that chapter. A narrative like this is to my mind one of the great proofs of the inspiration of Scripture. When I read the story of Bethany, I feel, "There is something here that the nonbeliever can never account for." — "This is nothing else but the finger of God."

The words I especially dwell on in John 11 are singularly moving and instructive. They record the message that Martha and Mary sent to Jesus when their brother Lazarus was sick: "Lord, the one you love is sick." That message was short and simple. Yet almost every word is deeply suggestive.

I invite the attention of my readers to the subject of sickness. The subject is one we ought frequently to look in the face. We cannot avoid it. It needs no prophet's eye to see sickness coming to each of us in turn one day. "In the midst of life we are in death." Let us take a few moments to consider sickness as Christians. The consideration will not hasten its coming, and by God's blessing, it may teach us wisdom.

In considering the subject of sickness, three points appear to me to demand attention. On each I will say a few words.

1. The *universal prevalence* of sickness and disease
2. The *general benefits* that sickness confers on mankind
3. The *special duties* to which sickness calls us

1. Universal Prevalence of Sickness

I need not dwell long on this point. To elaborate the proof of it would only be multiplying truisms accepted by all. Sickness is everywhere. In Europe, in Asia, in Africa, in America; in hot countries and in cold; in civilized nations and among savage tribes—men, women, and children get sick and die.

Sickness is known in all classes. Grace does not lift a believer above the reach of it. Riches will not buy exemption from it. Rank cannot prevent its assaults. Kings and their subjects, masters and servants, rich men and poor, learned and unlearned, teachers and scholars, doctors and patients, ministers and hearers—all alike go down before this great foe. "The wealth of the rich is their fortified city" (Proverbs 18:11). The Englishman's house is called his castle, but there are no doors and bars that can keep out disease and death.

Sickness is not preventable by anything that anyone can do. The average duration of life may doubtless be somewhat lengthened. The skill of doctors may continually discover new remedies and bring about surprising cures. The enforcement of wise sanitary regulations may greatly lower the death rate in a land. But, after all, whether in healthy or unhealthy localities, whether in mild climates or in cold, whether treated by alternative medicine or mainstream medicine, men and women will sicken and die. "Our days may come to seventy years, or eighty, if our strength endures; yet the best of them are but trouble and sorrow, for they quickly pass, and we fly away" (Psalm 90:10). That witness is indeed true. It was true thirty-three hundred years ago. It is true still.

The universal prevalence of sickness is one of the indirect evidences that the Bible is true. The Bible explains it. The Bible answers the questions about it that will arise in every inquiring mind. No other systems of religion can do this. They all fail here. They are silent. They are confounded. The Bible alone looks the subject in the face. It boldly proclaims the fact that man is a fallen creature, and with equal boldness it proclaims a vast remedial system to meet his wants. I feel compelled to the conclusion that the Bible is from God. Christianity is a revelation from heaven. "Your word is truth" (John 17:17).

2. General Benefits That Sickness Confers on Mankind

I use that word *benefits* advisedly. I believe it is profoundly important to see this part of our subject clearly. I know well that sickness is one of the supposed weak points in God's government of the world — an issue on which skeptical minds love to dwell. "Can God be a God of love when he allows pain? Can God be a God of mercy when he permits disease? He is able to prevent pain and disease — but he does not. How can these things be?" Such is the reasoning that often comes across the heart of mankind.

I know the suffering and pain that sickness entails. I admit the misery and wretchedness it often brings in its train. But I cannot regard it as an unmixed evil. I see in it a wise permission of God. I see in it a useful provision to check the ravages of sin and the devil among men and women's souls. If man had never sinned, I should have been at a loss to discern the benefit of sickness. But since sin is in the world, I can see that sickness is a good. It is a blessing quite as much as a curse. It is a rough schoolmaster, I grant. But it is a real friend to mankind's soul.

Sickness helps remind people of death. Most people live as if they were never going to die. They follow business, pleasure, politics, or science — as if earth were their eternal home. They plan and scheme for the future, like the rich fool in the parable, as if they have a long lease on life and are not tenants at will. A heavy illness sometimes goes far to dispel these delusions. It awakens people from their daydreams and reminds them that they have to die as well as to live. Now *this*, I say emphatically, is a mighty good.

Sickness helps make people think seriously about God and their souls and the world to come. Most people in their days of health can find no time for such thoughts. They dislike them. They put them away. They consider them to be troublesome and disagreeable. Now, a severe disease sometimes possesses a wonderful power to muster and rally these thoughts and place them before the eyes of a person's soul. Even a wicked king like Ben-Hadad, when he was sick, could think of Elisha (2 Kings 8:8). Even pagan sailors, when death was in sight, were afraid—and each cried to his own god (Jonah 1:5). Surely anything that helps make people think is a good.

Sickness helps soften people's hearts and teach them wisdom. The natural heart is as hard as a stone. It can see no good in anything that is not of this life and can imagine no happiness except as found in this world. A long illness sometimes goes far to correct these ideas. It exposes the emptiness and hollowness of what the world calls "good" things and teaches us to hold everything with a loose hand. The businessperson finds that money alone is not everything the heart requires. Those who love the world find that costly apparel, the reading of novels, and the glamour of parties and operas are miserable comforters in a sickroom. Surely anything that obliges us to alter the way we evaluate earthly things is a real good.

Sickness helps level and humble us. We are all naturally

proud and high-minded. Few, even among the poor, are free from the infection. Few are to be found who do not look down on somebody else and secretly flatter themselves that they are "not like other people." A sickbed is a mighty tamer of such thoughts as these. It forces on us the mighty truth that we are all poor worms, that we "live in houses of clay" and "are crushed more readily than a moth" (Job 4:19), and that kings and subjects, masters and servants, rich and poor, are all dying creatures who will soon stand side by side at the bar of God. In the sight of the coffin and the grave it is not easy to be proud. Surely anything that teaches that lesson is good.

Finally, sickness helps test people's religion to find out what kind it is. There are not many on earth who have no religion at all. Yet few have a religion that can bear inspection. Most are content with traditions received from their ancestors and can render no reason for the hope that they have. Now disease is sometimes profoundly useful to a person in exposing the utter worthlessness of their soul's foundation. It often shows them that they have nothing solid under their feet and nothing firm in their hand. It makes them realize that, although they may have had a form of religion, they have been worshiping "an unknown god" all their life. Surely anything that makes us discover the real character of our faith is a good.

We have no right to grumble about sickness and be discouraged about its presence in the world. We ought rather to thank God for it. It is God's witness. It is the soul's adviser. It is an awakener to the conscience. It is a purifier to the heart. Surely I have a right to tell you that sickness is a blessing and not a curse, a help and not an injury, a gain and not a loss, a friend and not a foe to mankind. As long as we have a world wherein there is sin, it is a mercy that it is a world wherein there is sickness.

3. Special Duties to Which the Prevalence of Sickness Calls Us

I would be remiss to leave the subject of sickness without saying something on this point. I hold it to be of utmost importance that I am not content with generalities in delivering God's message to souls. I am eager to impress on each one into whose hands this paper may fall their own personal responsibility in connection with the subject. In no way do I want anyone to finish this paper without being able to answer the questions, "What practical lesson have I learned? In a world of disease and death, what ought I to do?"

The prevalence of sickness calls us to always live in such a way that we are prepared to meet God. Sickness brings to the forefront of our minds the reality of death. Death is the door through which we must all pass to judgment. Judgment is the time when we must at last see God face-to-face. Surely the first lesson the inhabitant of a sick and dying world should learn is to prepare to meet his or her God.

I believe that this, and nothing less than this, is preparedness to meet God. Pardon of sin and equipped to be in God's presence, justification by faith and sanctification of the heart, the blood of Christ sprinkled on us and the Spirit of Christ dwelling in us — these are the grand essentials of the Christian religion. These are no mere words and names to furnish bones of contention for wrangling theologians. These are sober, solid, substantial realities. To live in the actual possession of these things in a world full of sickness and death is the first duty I press deep into your soul.

The prevalence of sickness calls us to always live in such a way that we will bear it patiently. Sickness is no doubt a trying thing to flesh and blood. To feel our nerves unstrung and our natural strength declining, to be obliged to sit still and be cut off from all our usual avocations, to see our plans broken off and our purposes disappointed, to endure long hours and days and nights of weariness and pain—all this is a severe strain on our sinful human nature. No wonder irritability and impatience are brought out by disease! Surely in such a dying world as this we should practice patience.

The prevalence of sickness calls us to always be ready to feel with and help our fellow human beings. Sickness is never very far from us. Few are the families who don't have some relative who battles sickness. Few are the parishes in which you won't find someone who is ill. But wherever there is sickness, there is a call to duty. A little timely assistance in some cases and a kindly visit in others, a friendly inquiry and a simple expression of compassion—these may do a vast good. These are the sort of things that soften rough edges, bring people together, and promote good feelings. These are ways by which you may ultimately lead people to Christ and save their souls. These are good deeds every professing Christian should be ready to do. In a world full of sickness and disease, we ought to "carry each other's burdens" and "be kind and compassionate to one another" (Galatians 6:2; Ephesians 4:32). If you can live in a sick and dying world and not feel for others, you have much yet to learn.

Practical Application

And now I conclude with four words of practical application. I want the subject of this paper to be turned to some spiritual use. My heart's desire, and my prayer to God, is that it will do good to souls.

1. As God's ambassador, I direct a question to all who read this paper, and I urge them to pay serious attention to it. It is a question that grows naturally out of the subject on which I have been writing. It is a question that concerns all—of every rank, class, and condition. I ask you, *What will you do when you are ill?* The time will come when you, as well as others, must go down the dark valley of the shadow of death. The hour will come when you, like your ancestors, must become sick and die. The time may be near or far off. God only knows. But whenever that time may be, I ask again, *What are you going to do? Where will you turn for comfort? On what will you rest your soul? On what will you build your hope? Where will you find your solace?*

2. I offer counsel to all who feel they need it and are willing to take it, to all who feel they are not yet prepared to meet God. That counsel is short and simple. *Acquaint yourself with the Lord Jesus Christ without delay. Repent, be converted, flee to Christ, and be saved.* You either have a soul or you don't. You will surely never deny that you have one. So then, if you have a soul, seek that soul's salvation. Of all the gambling in the world, there is none as reckless as that of the person who lives

in such a way that they are not prepared to meet God and who yet puts off repentance. You either have sins or you don't. If you have (and who dares to deny it?), let go of those sins, throw away your transgressions, turn away from them without delay. Either you need a Savior or you do not.

Vague, indefinite, and indistinct religion may do very well in time of health. It will never do in the day of sickness. A mere formal, perfunctory church membership may carry a person through the sunshine of youth and prosperity. It will break down entirely when death is in sight. Nothing will do then but real heart union with Christ. Christ interceding for us at God's right hand, Christ known and believed as our priest, our physician, our friend—Christ alone can rob death of its sting and enable us to face sickness without fear. He alone can deliver those who through fear of death are in bondage. I say to everyone who wants advice—*be acquainted with Christ.* If ever you would desire to have hope and comfort on the bed of sickness, be acquainted with Christ. Seek Christ. Draw near to Christ.

3. I exhort all true Christians who read this paper to remember how much they may glorify God in the time of sickness, and to be willing to lie quietly in God's hand when they are ill. I urge all sick believers to remember that they may honor God as much by patient suffering as by active work. It often shows more grace to sit still than it does to roam to and fro and perform great exploits. I beg them to remember that Christ cares for them as much when they are sick as he does when they are well, and that the very admonishing they feel so acutely is sent in love and not in anger.

Above all, I urge them to recall the compassion of Jesus for all his weak members. They are always tenderly cared for by him, but never so much as in their time of need. Jesus has had profound personal experience with sickness. He knows the heart of a sick person. He saw "every disease and sickness" (Matthew 10:1) when he was on earth. He was drawn especially to the sick in the days of his flesh. He still feels a special bond to them today. Sickness and suffering, I often think, make believers more like their Lord in experience than health does. "He took up our infirmities and bore our diseases" (Matthew 8:17). The Lord Jesus was a "man of suffering, and familiar with pain" (Isaiah 53:3). None have such an opportunity of learning the mind of a suffering Savior as suffering disciples.

4. I conclude with a word of exhortation to all believers, which I heartily pray that God will impress on their souls. I implore you to keep up a habit of close communion with Christ and to never be afraid of going too far in your religion. Remember this if you wish to have "great peace" in your times of sickness (Psalm 119:165). If you and I want to be "greatly encouraged" in our time of need, we must not be content with a bare union with Christ (Hebrews 6:18). We must seek to know something of heartfelt, experimental communion with him. Never, never let us forget that union is one thing, and communion another. Thousands, I fear, who know what *union* with Christ is know nothing of *communion*.

The day may come when, after a long fight with disease, we will feel that medicine can do no more and that nothing remains but to die. Friends will be standing by, unable to help us. Hearing, eyesight, even the power of prayer, will be fast failing us. The world and its shadows will be melting beneath our feet. Eternity, with its realities, will be looming large before our minds. What will support us in that trying hour? What will enable us to feel, "I will fear no evil" (Psalm 23:4)? Nothing, nothing can do it but close communion with Christ. Christ dwelling in our hearts by faith, Christ putting his right arm under our heads, Christ felt to be sitting by our side—Christ can alone give us the complete victory in the last struggle.

Let us cling to Christ more closely, love him more heartily, live to him more thoroughly, copy him more exactly, confess him more boldly, follow him more fully. Religion like this will always bring its own reward. Worldly people may laugh at it. Weak brothers and sisters may think it extreme. But it will wear well. As evening comes, it will bring us light. In sickness, it will bring us peace. In the world to come, it will give us "the crown of glory that will never fade away" (1 Peter 5:4).

In the meantime, let us live a life of faith in the Son of God. Let us lean all our weight on Christ and rejoice in the thought that he lives forever. Yes, blessed be God! Christ lives, though we may die. Christ lives, though friends and families are carried to the grave. He lives "who has destroyed death and has brought life and immortality to light through the gospel" (2 Timothy 1:10). He lives who said, "I will deliver this people from the power of the grave; I will redeem them from death" (Hosea 13:14). He lives who will one day "transform our lowly bodies so that they will be like his glorious body" (Philippians 3:21). In sickness and in health, in life and in death, let us lean confidently on him. Surely we ought to say daily with those of old, "Blessed be God for Jesus Christ!"

BIBLIOGRAPHY

Baxter, Richard. *The Reformed Pastor*. 1656. Reprint, Edinburgh: Banner of Truth, 2001.

Carson, D. A. *A Call to Spiritual Reformation: Priorities from Paul and His Prayers*. Grand Rapids: Baker, 1992.

Dickson, David. *The Elder and His Work*. 1883. Reprint, Phillipsburg, NJ: P & R, 2004.

Piper, John. "Hello, My Father Just Died." Posted March 6, 2007. Online, www.desiringgod.org/resource-library/taste-see-articles/hello-my-father-just-died. (Accessed October 21, 2013.)

Prime, Derek, and Alistair Begg. *On Being a Pastor: Understanding Our Calling and Work*. Chicago: Moody, 2004.

Spurgeon, Charles Haddon. *An All-Round Ministry*. 1900. Reprint, Edinburgh: Banner of Truth, 1960.

Spurgeon, C. H., Susannah Spurgeon, and W. J. Harrald. *C. H. Spurgeon's Autobiography*. Volume 1. 1899. Reprint, Pasadena, TX: Pilgrim, 1992.

Thomas, Curtis. *Practical Wisdom for Pastors: Words of Encouragement and Counsel for a Lifetime of Ministry*. Wheaton, IL: Crossway, 2001.

Whitney, Don. "Ten Questions to Ask to Turn a Conversation Toward the Gospel." Online, http://biblicalspirituality.org/wp-content/uploads/2011/02/Ten-questions-to-ask.pdf. (Accessed October 21, 2013.)

NOTES

1. Richard Baxter, *The Reformed Pastor* (1656; repr., Edinburgh: Banner of Truth, 2001), 102.
2. Charles Haddon Spurgeon, *An All-Round Ministry* (1900; repr., Edinburgh: Banner of Truth, 1960), 384.
3. David Dickson, *The Elder and His Work* (1883; repr., Phillipsburg, NJ: P & R, 2004), 58.
4. Ibid., 59.
5. This question *must* be followed up with some type of "why" question. For example, "Why do you believe God would allow you into heaven?" Answers that resemble "because I've been a good person"; "because God is loving"; "because I was baptized"; or "I hope [think] God will allow me into heaven" reveal they do not know the gospel. You must assess this first to be able to direct the rest of a spiritual conversation accordingly. See appendix 2 for examples of spiritual conversations.
6. Baxter, *Reformed Pastor*, 104.
7. D. A. Carson, *A Call to Spiritual Reformation: Priorities from Paul and His Prayers* (Grand Rapids: Baker, 1992), 33.
8. Curtis Thomas, *Practical Wisdom for Pastors: Words of Encouragement and Counsel for a Lifetime of Ministry* (Wheaton, IL: Crossway, 2001), 104.

9. Derek Prime and Alistair Begg, *On Being a Pastor: Understanding Our Calling and Work* (Chicago: Moody, 2004), 175.

10. Dickson, *Elder and His Work*, 60 (italics in the original).

11. Ibid.

12. Baxter, *Reformed Pastor*, 103.

13. Dickson, *Elder and His Work*, 60 – 61.

14. John Piper, "Hello, My Father Just Died," March 6, 2007, www.desiringgod.org/resource-library/taste-see-articles/hello-my-father-just-died (accessed October 21, 2013).

15. Dickson, *Elder and His Work*, 59.

16. C. H. Spurgeon, Susannah Spurgeon, and W. J. Harrald, *C. H. Spurgeon's Autobiography* (1899; repr., Pasadena, TX: Pilgrim, 1992), 1:371.

17. Ibid., 372.

18. Ibid., 371.